BARBRA STREISAND

" QUOTE UNQUOTE "

BARBRA STREISAND

" QUOTE UNQUOTE "

Derek Winnert

CRESCENT
BOOKS
New York • Avenel

ACKNOWLEDGEMENTS

The author and publisher acknowledge the following references, where many of the quotes in the book can be found: *The First Decade: The Films and Career of Barbra Streisand* by James Spada, *Barbra: The Second Decade* by Karen Swenson, *The Barbra Streisand Scrapbook* by Allison J Waldman, *Barbra Streisand* by William Ruhlman, *The Greatest Star: The Barbra Streisand Story* by Rene Jordan, *Barbra Streisand: The Untold Story* by Nelly Bly, *Barbra: An Actress Who Sings* by James Kimbrell, *Her Name Is Barbra* by Randall Reise, *Barbra: A Biography of Barbra Streisand* by Donald Zec & Antony Fowles, *Streisand: The Intimate Biography* by James Spada, *Variety*, *The Motion Picture Guide*, *The Great Movie Stars: The International Years* by David Shipman.

PICTURE ACKNOWLEDGEMENTS

Ronald Grant Archive: Back cover, 2, 12, 14, 16, 18, 20, 22, 23, 24, 28, 30, 31, 32, 34, 35, 37, 38, 40, 41, 42, 44, 46, 48, 49, 50, 53, 54, 56, 58, 59, 70, 72, 73, 75, 78 **Retna**: Everett Collection 8, 26; © Steve Granitz 19, 64; © Walter McBride 60, 63, 67; © Michael Benabib 65; © Bill Davila 66 **Redferns**: 68; Bob Willoughby 6, 13; Ebet Roberts 77 **London Features International**: Front Cover.

This 1996 edition is published by Crescent Books,
a division of Random House Value Publishing, Inc.,
40 Engelhard Avenue, Avenel, New Jersey 07001.

Crescent Books and colophon are registered trademarks of Random House Value Publishing, Inc.

Random House
New York ● Toronto ● London ● Sydney ● Auckland

First published in the UK in 1996
Copyright © Parragon Book Service Ltd 1996

ISBN: 0-517-18450-8
8 7 6 5 4 3 2 1

A CIP catalog record for this book is available from the Library of Congress

Produced by Haldane Mason, London
Editor: Paul Barnett
Design: Errol Campbell
Picture Research: Charles Dixon-Spain

Printed in Italy

CONTENTS

SHOW GIRL

'It wasn't that long ago I was sitting in
a candy store in Brooklyn eating ice cream
and reading movie magazines. Now all of
a sudden I'm appearing before those very
stars — and I'm now one of them.'

FACING PAGE: *Star gazing.*

One of the hits that Barbra Streisand sang in her 1960s breakthrough show – and in her subsequent smash-hit debut movie *Funny Girl* (1968) – was 'I'm The Greatest Star'. It was an appropriate title, because today Streisand does indeed have a serious claim to being 'the greatest star', certainly in her own sphere of musical comedy and emotional

BELOW: 'I'm the greatest star': getting ahead in a hat.

drama. She has few rivals in this particular field of show business which, though it enjoys a fanatical and widespread following, has fallen out of mainstream fashion through the effects of the various succeeding trends of pop music and youth culture since the teen revolution of the mid-1950s and the advent of rock'n'roll. Only Bette Midler, Liza Minnelli, Diana Ross, Bernadette Peters and Cher have claims to be her peers, and all of these artistes have had the most erratic of movie careers: great entertainers though they are, secure among the biggest draws on stage and recording, they do not possess Streisand's movie magnetism. Even her duds like *The Main Event* (1979) have been money-spinners. In this area only she can 'open a picture', as they say in the United States, or have lines forming outside the movie theatre on opening day.

Among the world's most notable performers and having spent 35 years in show business, Streisand is one of a handful of surviving Broadway musical legends. She is still an important movie star – despite long gaps between pictures – as well as a peerless light-comedy performer and a powerful dramatic actress. Her voice remains a magical musical instrument, and her albums continue to sell like hot cakes.

Unfortunately, though, she has an aversion to live performing. Apparently this is because of late-developing stage fright – a factor that seems to rule out her ever doing another stage musical. Happily, however, she has started doing live concerts again, albeit with carefully scripted dialogue and even the song lyrics being in front of her on an autocue. This has brought charges of a lack of spontaneity in her singing and performing, but the technical brilliance of her voice is undisputed – though once again hostile critics complain that she relies too much on technique and too little on heart and feeling in her performances. So much for the critics: the fans have little time for such carping, and just revel in the show!

Like the movie stars of the 1950s and 1960s – the period when she was forming her own ideas and personality – Streisand is one of the most powerful, influential women in showbiz: she can make her own deals as producer/ director/star, and is thus able to create a kind of movie comparatively rare in the modern Hollywood: pictures for grown-ups, with adult stories – not to mention

musicals in an era when they have all but disappeared. Indeed, she is probably the only star with the clout to assemble a movie musical today, when her nearest rivals – Midler, Minnelli and Ross – cannot. As Midler found with *For the Boys* (1991) and the Disney organization with *Newsies* (1992), the musical is the most precarious sort of picture you can try to make in the 1990s, both because it is expensive and because it appeals to an audience who normally see their movies on television. Streisand has frustratingly not attempted one since 1983's *Yentl*.

Professionally, this feminist-oriented star is frequently criticized for being 'difficult' and a 'control freak', and some of her famous male co-stars have had less than complimentary things to say about her. Her close friends and respected colleagues, by contrast, speak highly and warmly of her. She replies that she is simply a perfectionist and that these charges would not be laid against her if she were a man – what are called vices in an actress would be thought virtues in an actor.

Aside from her fanatical following among the family audience, she has a large number of gay fans, who regard her as a 'gay diva' (although she is not in fact

gay). She is recognized as a strong woman who has succeeded against the odds, having triumphed over less than perfect looks (which she has refused to correct with plastic surgery) and a lack of family fortune or connections. Oddly, she has had more than her fair share of critics, and some of the abuse is unpleasantly personal – focusing, for example, on her large nose, as if that were important.

But the real measure of Streisand is that her admirers are every bit as fanatical as her detractors.

The future 'greatest star' was born Barbara Joan Streisand in the working-class area of Brooklyn, New York, on April 24, 1942. Despite her blue eyes and her striking cheekbones, she was a plain girl (not helped by the fact that she was, apparently, bald until she was two), with a large, irregular nose and a huge mouth. But she soon proved to be talented, clever and ambitious, and from an early age she was stage-struck.

She suffered an extremely unhappy childhood, being raised by her dispirited mother Diana after Barbra's father had died, on August 4, 1943, aged 35, of respiratory failure following an epileptic seizure. The family's circumstances were

'We were poor, but not poor poor. We just never had anything.'

basic ('We were poor, but not poor poor. We just never had anything'). Describing her mother many years later, Streisand said: 'She's mainly interested in basic things like eating and breathing. She's a very secure person, sort of like, uh, normal.'

In the summer of 1949 her mother remarried. In the emotionally abusive treatment he meted out to the Streisand family Barbra's stepfather scarcely lived up to his name: Louis Kind.

The sensitive, shy, lonely young Streisand went to Erasmus High School in Brooklyn, which she disliked, though she graduated in January 1959 with a medal in Spanish. The movie-mad teenager got her first taste of showbiz when she spent her 1957 school vacation working in summer stock at the Malden Bridge Playhouse, New York. After graduation, she moved to Manhattan and found theatre work of a sort: sweeping up at the Cherry Lane Theatre. Crashing out wherever she could, she studied under two drama coaches in return for performing babysitting duties. She also took work as a switchboard girl and a cinema usherette, all the time dreaming of being a glamorous showbiz star.

Discouragingly, a long series of theatre auditions produced nothing but rejections. Still, her ambition drove her on to sing in an amateur talent contest in Manhattan's Greenwich Village in Spring 1961. Here she had an instant success, which led to a short hit engagement and soon landed her nightclub spots. Her second step up the ladder of fame came when she made her first television appearance, on April 5, 1961, on *The Jack Paar Show*.

At this point she was a young woman in a hurry, and everything was happening very quickly for her. Showbiz people recognized her obvious talent, while a

'She's mainly interested in basic things like eating and breathing. She's a very secure person, sort of like, uh, normal.'

ON HER MOTHER

RIGHT: Barbra in costume for the 1961 off-Broadway revue Another Evening with Harry Stoones.

growing public warmed to her gorgeous voice and the appealing kookie stage personality she had already developed.

Her third rung on the ladder should have been her appearance in a daffy off-Broadway revue called *Another Evening with Harry Stoones,* starring Dom DeLuise. But, devastatingly, it opened and closed on the same night — Saturday October 21, 1961 — a casualty of the bad reviews that it would receive in the Monday-morning papers.

Despite this setback, she soon landed a small part as Yetta Tessye Marmelstein in the moderately successful Broadway show *I Can Get It for You Wholesale* (which opened on March 22, 1962); she got rave personal reviews and won the New York Critics' Award. Against the wishes of the show's director Arthur Laurents, she insisted on singing sitting down: 'Do it in your goddamned chair, it's your funeral,' said Laurents, but in fact Streisand was accorded a standing ovation on opening night at the tryout in Philadelphia. 'I couldn't understand why they were mad at me for being right,' Streisand later remarked.

The show's original-cast album became her first LP; on it she sings four songs, including the comic showstopper 'Miss Marmelstein'.

'I couldn't understand why they were mad at me for being right.'

Things were going fine in her personal life, too. She rapidly fell in love with the show's handsome leading man, Elliott Gould, and they were married on September 13, 1963, in Carson City. She was just 21 and he was 25. It looked at the time as though this would be a fairytale story with a happy-ever-after ending. She was a hit in New York supper clubs like the Bon Soir and the Blue Angel and in further television appearances like *Mike Wallace's PM East* and *The Garry Moore Show*.

On the music front everything was on song. In 1963 she landed a megabucks recording contract with Columbia Records, and cut *The Barbra Streisand Album* and *The Second Barbra Streisand Album* in quick succession. Both of these were well reviewed and became big worldwide hits, initiating a long line of albums that has by now entered its fourth decade.

Then, early in 1964, came her major breakthrough. Powerful producer Ray Stark offered her the lead role – playing the famed 1930s Ziegfeld Follies musical comedy star Fanny Brice – in Jule Styne's and Bob Merrill's Broadway musical *Funny Girl*, as replacement for the originally cast Anne Bancroft. The show

LEFT: Streisand and her leading man, Elliott Gould: they married in September 1963.

opened at New York's Winter Garden theatre on March 26, 1964, and was a huge success. *Village Voice* said: 'She represents a remarkable and rare meeting between a common touch that leads us all to identify with her and a showbiz sheen that makes her our ideal.' Sydney Chaplin co-starred as her jailed husband Nick Arnstein, with Kay Medford as Mrs Brice and Jean Stapleton as Mrs Strakosh. The long roster of hit songs included several classics, like 'People', 'Don't Rain On My Parade', 'You Are Woman, I Am Man', 'Sadie Sadie', 'I'm The Greatest Star' and 'His Love Makes Me Beautiful', plus some songs that had already become famous, notably 'My Man', 'Second Hand Rose' and 'I'd Rather Be Blue Over You'.

Finding herself the toast of the town, Streisand was nominated for a Broadway Tony Award as Best Musical Actress. In the event she lost to Carol Channing, who won the award for her role in *Hello, Dolly!* The disappointment may have helped fire Streisand's ambition to star in the movie version of the latter when it was made in 1968.

Funny Girl ran with Streisand in the lead for nearly two years, and continued for a further year after she quit, on December 25, 1965, in order to re-create the role in London's West End. It opened there on April 13, 1966, for a sell-out 14 weeks at the Prince of Wales Theatre. Barbra arrived to find the ancient star dressing room tiny and tatty — unsuitable for a Broadway stage superstar — and asked for it to be refurbished. Two dressing rooms were quickly knocked into one for her.

Among the long line of stars who called on her during the London run was Sophia Loren, who said: 'I would give anything if I could sing like you.' Streisand replied: 'If I could look like you I wouldn't even wanna talk.'

> *'I would give anything if I could sing like you.'*
> SOPHIA LOREN

Streisand was also introduced to the Queen, who told her: 'I have all your records.' Overcome, Streisand could only say: 'Yeah?'

There was an avalanche of praise, but it has to be admitted that not all the reviews were ecstatic. *The Times* pronounced: 'Streisand makes one temporarily accept one of the most nonsensical plots in the history of the American musical . . . Playing anything but comedy she is dull . . . What she does project is the same force of personality which must have carried Fanny Brice to the top.'

Nevertheless, *Funny Girl* was a sensation, and she was now the talk of London. But, having spent so long in the show on Broadway, she soon wearied of whole thing, telling her UK co-star Michael Craig: 'Two and a half years ago when I started this show in Philadelphia it was so much fun and everything was marvellous. Now it's all so difficult and I don't get any fun out of it any more.'

Disappointingly for her stage fans, she was so put off by the repetitive slog of long runs, while at the same time being fired by an ambition to make movies ('being a star means being a movie star'), that this was the last time she ever appeared as a performer in legitimate theatre.

If life had become boring in London, it certainly wasn't when she got back home. Six months after the end of the London run her son Jason Emanuel Gould was born, on December 29, 1966.

> *'If I could look like you I wouldn't even wanna talk.'*
> TO SOPHIA LOREN

MOVIE STAR

'I don't know what other actresses do. Do they just sorta stand around like mummies, get dressed, get told what to do, move here, move there? That can be pretty boring for the actress and the director, besides what it does or does not do for the performance.'

FACING PAGE: Walter Matthau and Barbra in Hello, Dolly!

Back in the United States, Streisand's career swung into an up-gear. She began to appear regularly as a prized guest on top-rated television shows, thereby making her name with the general public rather than just among New York show-goers. Programmes included *The Jack Paar Show*, *Mike Wallace's PM East* and *The David Susskind Show*. Barbra followed these guest slots with appearances on prime-time television shows like those fronted by Dinah Shore, Garry Moore and Ed Sullivan and, memorably, took part in a

My Name Is Barbra

RIGHT: The record of the show: Barbra's first TV special in 1965 wins five Emmy awards.

Bob Hope special in 1963. She followed this up by performing even more famously, on October 6, 1963, in *The Judy Garland Show*. Despite everyone's jitters, Garland and Streisand worked beautifully together, particularly in a duet suggested by Garland, with Barbra singing 'Happy Days' and Judy belting out 'Get Happy'. The duo were joined by Ethel Merman for 'There's No Business Like Show Business', with Ethel's auditorium-filling voice effectively swamping the others. But it was definitely Barbra's evening, and she was nominated for an Emmy for an outstanding musical performance – the first time any television-show guest had been so honoured.

Then, early in 1964, she picked up a $5 million contract with CBS for a series of television specials. These started auspiciously with *My Name is Barbra* on April 28, 1965, which won five Emmys, including those for Outstanding Program and Individual Achievement in Entertainment for Streisand. *My Name is Barbra* was also important to Streisand's career in that it introduced her to the great US public in a format over which she had full artistic control – the show was produced by her own company.

There followed more successes: *Color Me Barbra* on March 30, 1966, and *The Belle of 14th Street* with Jason Robards (motoring on a freewheeling theme of the golden age of vaudeville) on October 11, 1967.

Before this last show came her free concert in Manhattan Central Park on June 16, 1967, performed before a crowd of 135,000 and lasting two and a half hours. This was televised in colour as her fourth special, called *A Happening in Central Park,* but by now Streisand had decided that she wanted to concentrate

on pursuing a Hollywood career, and her television appearances began to tail off.

The television specials had done what she wanted them to — establish her name with the public at large — and now it was time to do more challenging and lasting work. In 1971 she did guest on an Emmy-winning *Burt Bacharach Special,* but she delayed the making of her fifth television special, *Barbra Streisand . . . And Other Musical Instruments.* By the time it was screened — on November 2, 1973 — she was long-established as a major movie star.

Streisand had been movie-struck since the late 1950s, when this lonely teenager had become infatuated with the films starring Gregory Peck, Marlon Brando, Elizabeth Taylor and Audrey Hepburn that she saw in her local movie theatre. Now, in the mid-1960s, having conquered the worlds of stage, recording and television, she yearned to scale the Hollywood heights. Soon the girl from Brooklyn was going to be mingling with these superstars and become one of them. In 1965 — the year in which she said, 'To me, being a star means being a movie star' — Barbra became the first star to sign for four pictures without having ever stepped onto a movie set.

She rightly saw her Broadway/London hit show as her first stepping stone to screen success. Veteran director William Wyler's movie version of *Funny Girl* (1968) was her first film; it was produced by Wyler and by her stage mentor Ray Stark. As seems almost always the way in Hollywood, Columbia Pictures did not initially want the stage lead to take the movie role, preferring the idea of an established star like Shirley MacLaine, but Stark, with whom Streisand had signed the four-movie contract, held out firmly for Barbra. Columbia capitulated, though with

BELOW: Streisand wins an Oscar as Fanny Brice in the movie version of Funny Girl.

the proviso that the movie was to be made on a tight budget, for a musical, of $8.5 million (compared with her next movie *Hello Dolly!* which cost more than $20 million).

Sidney Lumet had originally been set to direct, but he had left the project because of artistic differences. It was then that Columbia proposed Wyler, who had helmed a recent hit for them with the psychological thriller *The Collector* (1966), based on the bestselling John Fowles novel. Though Wyler, then 66 and a three-time Oscar-winner – for *Mrs Miniver* (1942), *The Best Years of Our Lives* (1946) and *Ben-Hur* (1959) – was known as a sympathetic 'women's director', having steered another very positive actress, Bette Davis, successfully through *Jezebel* (1938) and *The Little Foxes* (1941), surprisingly he had never directed a musical before (perhaps because he was deaf in one ear). Streisand was dubious about him, but agreed to work with him when she was informed that Samantha Eggar had won an Oscar nomination as Best Actress for *The Collector*.

Next Herbert Ross was signed as the director and choreographer of the 16 musical numbers that make up nearly an hour of *Funny Girl's* 155 minutes. Wyler and Ross combined to form an expert, complementary team – and Ross was clearly especially compatible with Barbra, since he went on to direct two other Streisand movies, becoming the only director other than herself to helm more than one of her pictures.

The behind-the-camera team was completed by the veteran MGM cine-matographer Harry Stradling. He had worked on *My Fair Lady* (1964) and had a reputation for bringing out the best in a star's appearance; this was an especially important concern of Barbra's, because she was insecure about her looks, partic-ularly after Columbia's palaver about whether or not they would translate effectively to the big screen.

Funny Girl's all-important team seems, when we look back at it now, to have been assembled rather haphazardly – a common pattern in Hollywood, as the various players are assembled, fall by the wayside, take other players with them and are replaced to form the final pack-age of a movie – but it was exactly right on the night.

They got the performers right, too. Omar Sharif was chosen to take on the role of sophisticated gambler Nick Arnstein; although some found him an odd choice, the casting proved to be ideal. Veteran MGM star Walter Pidgeon played the old showman Florenz Ziegfeld, while Kay Medford re-created her stage role as Mrs Brice. Somewhat unusually for movie versions of musicals, *Funny Girl* is true to the spirit of the show and the original Broadway score, though a couple of useful additions came from the show's songwriters, Jule Styne

---

'Miss Streisand's talent is very poignant and strong, but the movie almost does her in.'
NEW YORK TIMES ON FUNNY GIRL

---

and Bob Merrill, in the form of 'Roller Skate Rag' and the title tune.

Resolutely old-fashioned at a time of great change, when the new youth cul-ture was burgeoning in the United States and across the world, *Funny Girl* caught on with the public and took $22 million at the US box office, though Barbra her-self was paid only $250,000. A personal triumph for her, it landed her a shared Best Actress Oscar, the first time since

ABOVE: A shoulder to rely on: Egyptian actor Omar Sharif is picked as Barbra's Funny Girl *co-star just before Egypt and Israel start a war.*

of a megaphone, saying, 'You should be a director.' The remark may have been made in the spirit of good fun, but it was undoubtedly not meant to be a compliment. Eventually, though, she was to take his advice at face value.

The reviews for this rousing musical tribute to showbiz's swings and roundabouts were deservedly good, particularly for Barbra's performance. *Variety* said: 'Streisand makes a marked impact . . . It is to the credit of all concerned that it plays so convincingly.' Yet, even from the very beginning of her movie career, Streisand has never been able to escape the sound of detractors sharpening their claws. Renata Adler's verdict on *Funny Girl* in the *New York Times* was curious: 'Miss Streisand's talent is very poignant and strong, but the movie almost does her in.' UK critic Dilys Powell, though, added her own praise for Barbra (in September 1970): 'Stars need the strength of steel. The newcomer Barbra Streisand looks as if she might have it.'

1932 that the award had been split; Streisand shared it with Katharine Hepburn, honoured for her role in *A Lion in Winter* (1968). Streisand was still only 26. However, the film's seven other nominations, including that for Best Picture, were disappointingly not translated into Oscars.

After the filming William Wyler, whom Barbra had not been afraid to advise on the shooting, made her the gift

Twentieth Century-Fox was in the mid-1960s – as it still is, 30 years later – pursuing the elusive 'family entertainment' market, and particularly was exploring the genre of musicals, which seemed to be having a renewed vogue.

The company had bought the movie rights to make one of the decade's most popular and long-running musicals – Jerry Herman's smash-hit show *Hello, Dolly!*, which in 1964 had starred on stage Carol Channing (who, we recall, had pipped Streisand to the post for the Tony Award that year). At various times after Channing's tenure, the stage version of *Hello, Dolly!* had provided an appropriate role for stars like Mary Martin, Betty Grable, Pearl Bailey and Ginger Rogers. All these redoubtable ladies would have been ideal casting for the Fox movie – artistically, at any rate: the box office might have been another matter. Channing herself simply was not a movie cash-register magnet: her rare movie appearance in *Thoroughly Modern Millie* (1967) around this time won her an Oscar nomination, but the film itself flopped badly, despite the fact that it starred Julie Andrews.

The success of the show and later the movie *Funny Girl* further emboldened the studio, which desperately wanted another musical hit of the magnitude of their beloved money-spinner *The Sound of Music* (1964). Eschewing the logic of likely casting, they gave the green light to the 26-year-old Streisand taking the lead in *Hello, Dolly!* (1969). This, only her second movie, was directed appropriately, and in considerable style, by veteran hoofer Gene Kelly.

There is no doubt that Barbra is in top voice in this movie, and she oozes charisma, but she was several decades too young to play the middle-aged, meddling

BELOW: 'Just leave everything to me': Barbra as the matchmaker Dolly Levi in Hello, Dolly!

ABOVE: Barbra serenading her beaux with one of the Oscar-winning songs in Hello, Dolly!

matchmaker Dolly Levi (the musical is based on Thornton Wilder's stage classic *The Matchmaker,* earlier filmed in 1958 with Shirley Booth as Dolly). The ambitious, good-looking production, perhaps the final fling of the old Hollywood studios, worryingly turned out to be a vastly expensive affair (estimated at $20–$24 million), with huge sets that you want to applaud but which cost a packet. For one number alone Fox transformed the whole outside of the studio lot into a single mammoth street scene of New York at the turn of the century.

This time Streisand was paid $750,000 plus a percentage – but it was still not much when you consider that the producer of the original Broadway show, David Merrick, took $2 million.

Hello, Dolly! turned out to be a good, solid, entertaining movie version of a classic Broadway musical, made with a loving, old-style craftsmanship that earned it Oscars for Best Art Direction, Best Sound and Best Adapted Score. Harry Stradling, who had done such a great job of photographing Barbra in *Funny Girl,* had rightly been asked back as cinematographer, and he produced further memorable images. Packed with musical highlights, the picture even found space for a guest appearance by Louis Armstrong, who had earlier enjoyed a Number One hit with the title song; here he joined Barbra in a restaurant sequence for a duet of the number.

One of the film's biggest successes was Walter Matthau, delightfully playing, in his inimitable fashion, the part of Streisand's reluctant love interest, the greedy, grouchy store owner Horace Vandergelder. ('On the cold winter nights, Horace, you can cuddle up to your cash register,' Streisand tells him in the movie. 'It's a little lumpy but it rings.') The show also starred UK actor Michael Crawford, then extremely callow and seemingly ill at ease with the song-and-dance numbers – ironic since, much later, the Andrew Lloyd Webber musical *The Phantom of the Opera* (1986) was to turn him into a famed international star of musicals and Barbra would perform a duet with him on her *Back to Broadway* album in 1993.

The original composer, Jerry Herman, provided two new songs for the film – 'Just Leave Everything To Me' and 'Love Is Only Love' – to add to the other tunes from the show, nearly all of them toe-tapping hits. Especially charming are 'Elegance', 'Put On Your Sunday Clothes', 'It Takes A Woman', 'So Long Dearie', 'It Only Takes A Moment' and, of course, the singalong title track.

Despite all these glorious bonuses, it turned out that musicals were (seemingly terminally) out of favour at the cinema box-office, and *Hello, Dolly!* took only $13 million in the United States – even though it garnered generally good reviews. As an example, this time *Variety* opined: 'Streisand is a unique performer with that inborn vitality which marks great personalities. She brings her own special kind of authority.'

But now the backbiting that has marked and marred Barbra's entire movie career had started. Her fellow performer Walter Matthau made no secret of his dislike for her. Although an undoubted asset to the film, Matthau became one of her many movie co-stars through the years who apparently have not always seen eye-to-eye with her: 'I had no disagreements with Barbra Streisand. I was merely exasperated at her tendency to become a complete megalomaniac,' he

---

'I had no disagreements with Barbra Streisand. I was merely exasperated at her tendency to become a complete megalomaniac.'
WALTER MATTHAU

---

said. The newspapers were at it too. The London *Sunday Times* declared: 'There's a market on late-night TV shows for anti-Streisand anecdotes. She scares people. She could be Madame Guillotine the way some people speak of her.' Meanwhile *Time* added: 'Streisand's mannerisms are

ABOVE: Cool, calm and talented – the actress of the decade according to her special Broadway Tony Award.

as 'Actress of the Decade'. Maybe Broadway was hoping to tempt her back, but, if so, the wish was in vain. She was seemingly lost to the stage, whether as an actress or as a concert artist: Hollywood and recording were her sole concerns.

Streisand unexpectedly and ill-advisedly turned to a risky project for her third

---

'There's a market on late-night TV shows for anti-Streisand anecdotes. She scares people. She could be Madame Guillotine the way some people speak of her.'
THE SUNDAY TIMES

---

so arch and calculated that one half-expects to find a key implanted in her back.' Notwithstanding the (often jealousy-propelled) gossip, she retained legions of supporters, and in 1970 she won a special Broadway Tony Award

film. This was another stage-to-film transfer of a Broadway show: *On a Clear Day You Can See Forever* (1970). Unlike the case with her first two movies, Alan Jay Lerner's and Burton Lane's show had enjoyed only a modest stage success (with Barbara Harris starring), and it is an oddball, rather unappealing story with only one show-stopping song – the title number – and at least superficially little else to recommend it. To add to the risks, producer Howard W. Koch engaged as director for the project the Hollywood veteran Vincente Minnelli. He had done wonderful work during MGM's glorious musical heyday – with *Meet Me in St Louis* (1944), *An American in Paris* (1951) and *The Band Wagon* (1953) – and had won an Oscar for *Gigi* (1958), but sadly turned out to be past his prime at 60; his last movie had been the awful Burton–Taylor romance *The Sandpiper* (1965), five years earlier.

Streisand is scarcely well cast as a chain-smoking heroine sent for a cure by her fiancé to a psychiatrist, who finds that under hypnosis she can whizz back to the 19th century, where she was a Cockney girl posing as a lady (in a theme Lerner had already explored with *My Fair Lady,* based on Shaw's play *Pygmalion).*

There has of course been struggle, but there have been few disappointments or setbacks in Streisand's irresistible progress. This time, though, it proved to be third movie unlucky for her. *On A Clear Day You Can See Forever* was nothing short of a disaster. Viewing it today is even more difficult than it was 25 years ago – although there were few people who willingly underwent the experience

at the time. For once the star looks silly, over made-up and dressed in the hippyish glad rags of 1970, though as always her professionalism sees her through and her singing is superb. Moreover, her renowned French co-star Yves Montand, who had been foolishly recommended to go for a Hollywood career, is terribly uncomfortable as both actor and singer, struggling through no fault of his own with a thick French accent which lacks the charm of, say, Boyer's or Chevalier's. Jack Nicholson is even more uncomfortable as Streisand's hippy, guitar-playing stepbrother, though the final print spared him the embarrassment of his awkward rendition of his solo song.

Minnelli let the movie slip through his fingers, though it was by no means his fault alone, since Lerner could not solve the script problems. Post-production editing left the film even weaker and scarcely coherent – all too obviously, several scenes ended up on the cutting-room floor – and it was a dismal box-office failure. Streisand had done the right thing in surrounding herself with the best talent, but she found that even the best talent has its off-days. The lesson she learnt was that, whenever she could, she should do it herself.

FUNNY GIRL

'Herbie, I can't. I've got goose bumps and they'll show. What will my mother think of this? I don't think I have that great a body. I don't think I'm ready for it.'
To THE OWL AND THE PUSSYCAT
DIRECTOR, HERBERT ROSS

FACING PAGE: The concert conclusion to A Star Is Born.

Shaken by the debacle of *On a Clear Day You Can See Forever*, Streisand — who had, after all, first established herself in her early television appearances at least partly as a kooky funny lady — cannily took the decision to switch to movie comedy. In this field she has achieved great success and public approbation. Her comedies have been carefully overseen by her regular producer since the stage version of *Funny Girl*, Ray Stark, an expert judge of the

RIGHT: *Skeleton service: Barbra's and George Segal's 'very today' movie* The Owl and the Pussycat *narrowly escaped the dreaded American X-rating.*

public fancy; the string of hits to his credit include *The Goodbye Girl* (1978), *Brighton Beach Memoirs* (1986) and *Steel Magnolias* (1989).

The first comic Streisand outing was the slightly risqué adult sex farce *The Owl and the Pussycat* (1970), based on a 1964 Broadway play written by Bill Manhoff which made a racial point by starring Alan Alda opposite black actress Diana Sands, but which was given a thorough overhaul for the cinema by screenwriter Buck Henry, who had co-written the screenplay for *The Graduate* (1967) and written solo that for *Catch-22* (1970). Streisand took on an altered role as a Brooklyn tart with a heart, playing opposite lovelorn Bronx bookstore clerk George Segal, who gave a vibrant, funny performance that matched Streisand's. The unlikely team clicked, displaying lots of charisma and sexual chemistry, with everything held together expertly by the director Herbert Ross, an ex-dance director now making good at the helm.

No doubt sticking to her game plan of staying with the best talent, Streisand next turned in 1972 to the then toast of Hollywood, Peter Bogdanovich, who had established his reputation with *Targets* (1967) and *The Last Picture Show* (1971).

In fact, Bogdanovich came into Streisand's life by a lucky and peculiar chance. In February 1971 Barbra's husband Elliott Gould had dropped out of making a film called *A Glimpse of Tiger*, with Kim Darby, due to an 'emotional breakdown'. Warners, oddly, rescheduled the film with Streisand and Ryan O'Neal, and approached Bogdanovich to direct. He rejected the offer when he read the screenplay, and *A Glimpse of Tiger* was never finished. But Bogdanovich said he would like to work with Streisand, who meanwhile had seen and admired *The Last Picture Show*. However, it turned out that the new movie, a 1930s-style screwball comedy (advertising line: 'A screwball comedy. Remember them?') was as far from the searing drama of *The Last Picture Show* as you could imagine, though ironically *The Last Picture Show* was just the sort of adult emotional movie that Streisand actually craved to make.

At any rate, the result was that she was lucky enough to follow *The Owl and the Pussycat* with one of producer/ director/story-writer Bogdanovich's best films, *What's Up, Doc?* (1972), in which she played opposite her friend O'Neal in what turned out to be a smash-hit

comedy. Clearly made in homage to the Katharine Hepburn-Cary Grant classic *Bringing Up Baby* (1938) — indeed, Bogdanovich screened the earlier movie for his two stars to show them what he wanted — it established a life and classic status of its own.

The story closely parallels that of *Bringing Up Baby,* as the scatterbrained, quick-talking heroine pursues the owlish, bespectacled hero, oblivious to his disdain and his fiancée (Madeline Kahn). The movie offers a riot of freewheeling

ABOVE: Women do make passes at men in glasses: Ryan O'Neal pays lip service to Barbra in What's Up, Doc?

ABOVE: Freewheeling laughs on the streets of San Francisco in What's Up, Doc?

laughs, and Bogdanovich gets the utmost fun out of his zany characters, crazy situations and well-chosen San Francisco locations. Again Buck Henry was among the screenplay credits; he was brought in by Bogdanovich to rewrite the original script the director had commissioned (and disliked) by Robert Benton and David Newman.

Variety proclaimed *What's Up, Doc?* 'a total smash', and Rex Reed said Streisand was 'a nimble comedienne who is especially winning when she lounges atop a piano mimicking Humphrey Bogart and singing "As Time Goes By"'. But still some critics took up cudgels against her. *Newsweek,* for example, attacked with: 'Unlike Katharine Hepburn, gossamer charm is not Miss Streisand's long suit. When Hepburn was cunning, Miss Streisand tracking O'Neal smells of desperation.' Streisand herself, hungry for meaningful work and wanting to be taken seriously as an actress, had grave reservations: 'What is it about? I'll tell you what it's about – nothing!'

On the private front, things weren't going so well. Barbra's relationship with husband Elliott Gould had long been under strain, since both were in the glare of the public eye and in private analysis, while constantly enduring the pressures of ambitiously pursuing high-profile but unequal movie careers. During the filming of *Funny Girl* Gould had stopped his own work to help manage Barbra's business affairs, but when he had gone to New York to make *The Night They Raided Minsky's* (1968) she had stayed at home in Hollywood, where the rumour was that she had become romantically involved with Omar Sharif; whether it was true or not, the rumour obviously didn't help the marriage.

Yet this was only a part of it. Basically, Gould seemed unable to cope with the extent of Streisand's success and fame, and the frustrations of his relatively modest career. In a reflection of the situation in *A Star is Born* (1937) — which Barbra was to refilm in 1976 — Gould resented being known simply as Mr Barbra Streisand. Also, as he stated at the

---

'Barbra lives her life worrying about what people think of her, not only how she performs but how she looks.'
ELLIOTT GOULD

---

time: 'Barbra lives her life worrying about what people think of her, not only how she performs but how she looks.'

After an incident in which Gould punched a photographer who had been persistently bothering her, Barbra reluctantly decided to separate from him in February 1969, although initially neither of them wanted to divorce, hoping they could get back together again later,

particularly for the sake of their son Jason. But, early in 1971, she was seen in public dating Ryan O'Neal and, just before the new couple made their first picture together, Streisand was divorced from Gould, in June 1971.

Happy in her new relationship with the current Hollywood favourite O'Neal, Barbra made new strides in the industry, consolidating her power and control as a way of protecting herself and her career, and reaching out towards the more ambitious and intelligent film projects she craved to do. In 1969 she had become one of the film-producing powers behind First Artists Inc. — along with Paul Newman and Sidney Poitier, and later also with Steve McQueen and Dustin Hoffman.

Unfortunately for First Artists, Streisand then made the obscure comedy *Up the Sandbox* (1972) about a fantasizing Manhattan mother; it flopped. Streisand herself was deeply involved in the project ('I care about *Sandbox*. I think it is a provocative film and I want to help it'), and supported it with as much publicity as she could, but the public and critics disliked it. In truth, it was an exemplar of the kind of film that stars love to make (hostile commentators would call it

ABOVE: Shifting sands: Barbra as a fantasizing Manhattan mother in the 1972 flop Up the Sandbox.

a vanity project, sympathetic critics would call it brave) and which, in the golden days of Hollywood, studios kept their actors miles away from. That is not to say that such films may not be brave or thoughtful, just that they are risky – and costly when things go wrong.

Many years earlier, when actors Douglas Fairbanks Sr, Mary Pickford and Charles Chaplin had formed United Artists in 1919, the enterprise had been described as the 'lunatics taking over the

asylum', and many of the old-style Hollywood moguls would have thought the same about First Artists. *(Variety* worried about 'an undeniable threat to the uneasy status quo in Hollywood film-making'.) Their work would include such peculiarities as Steve McQueen's version of Henrik Ibsen's *An Enemy of the People* (1977) – just the sort of thing that people didn't want to see. Streisand herself was far too in tune with the audience to be caught with such a career-damaging entry on her resumé, but with *Up the Sandbox* she missed the popular pulse.

In a comment typical of the movie's general reception, *Variety* attacked *Up the Sandbox* as 'an untidy melange of over-produced, heavy-handed fantasy. Were Streisand to have been working off some old contractual commitment, there would be much sympathy. But this is not the case since the star is the producer'.

In 1973, back with her old producer Ray Stark, the mentor and father-figure with whom she had in 1965 done a deal for her first four pictures, Streisand scored a big hit with the intelligent, upmarket romantic comedy *The Way We Were* (1973), playing opposite golden boy Robert Redford. The film's serious-minded anatomy of a love affair and marriage meanders from the 1930s to the 1950s and is set against a background of political activism and the changing US political climate. Many people were surprised (and some mocked) that Barbra could take on the part of a college communist in the 1930s, not associating the star of escapist musicals with the realism of active politics (with hindsight, this was a misplaced view, given her later story). Critics complained that Redford's and the support roles were reduced to undeveloped ciphers, merely small-time courtiers in attendance to the Hollywood queen, but this objection came about in fact because jittery pre-release cuts had hacked back their parts and eliminated some of the film's most serious and thought-provoking elements.

Prestige Hollywood player Sydney Pollack had been brought in to co-produce and direct. The focus of his interest was probably the film's 1950s Hollywood blacklisting theme – making it all the more frustrating that it was this part of the movie that took the brunt of the cutting. Pollack is renowned for his large-canvas, sometimes unnecessarily long films, but on this occasion the under-two-hour running time could easily have stood an extra 20 minutes or so of

top material. The screenwriter Arthur Laurents, who had based the script on his own novel, was disappointed with the released film and disowned the final cut.

Critic John Simon led with his knife: 'Director Sydney Pollack has tried to tone down her brashness and shrillness, but has hardly made a dent in the basic pugnacious charmlessness that is beyond redemption. The difficulty is that even

ABOVE: The funny girl from Brooklyn and the golden boy from California in The Way We Were.

when Streisand labours to appear sensitive and vulnerable, she cannot conquer our impression that, were she to collide with a Mac truck, it is the truck that would drop dead.'

Variety didn't like this one either: 'The overemphasis on Streisand makes the film just another one of those Streisand vehicles where no other elements ever get a chance.' Indeed, particularly at this stage of his career, Redford might have wondered exactly what he was doing playing such an obvious second fiddle to Barbra — especially since producer/director Pollack was a long-time associate of his; they had first worked together on *This Property Is Condemned* back in 1966, and had just been doing another picture together, the semi-western *Jeremiah Johnson* (1972), a horse of a very different colour from *The Way We Were*.

Nevertheless, Streisand had worked minor wonders with her role, and she gained her reward when she secured an Oscar nomination as Best Actress — although, if the truth be told, by far the best thing about the movie was the Marvin Hamlisch music and title song (with lyrics by Alan Bergman and Marilyn Bergman). Streisand turned the

material into a great album, one of her finest. The cover picture shows a gorgeous-looking, red-lipped Streisand as Katie Morosky, head veiled in an impressively vast turban, every inch the old-fashioned movie star *à la* Lana Turner; the shot in question had in fact been deleted from the finished movie.

Producer Ray Stark's next outing for Streisand, *For Pete's Sake* (1974), was perhaps a mistake. A moderate, rather contrived comedy, this features a struggling Brooklyn housewife and her cabbie husband who are short of cash and use insider knowledge to invest money they don't have in pork bellies on the stock exchange. Not much of a plot — and not much of a title, either, under its initial monicker *July Pork Bellies!* (Its second title, *For the Love of Pete,* had been scarcely more promising.) The amiable Michael Sarrazin was chosen to co-star, because a big-name, equal-drawing actor was not required in what was a clearly subordinate part. The movie was directed by Peter Yates, an odd choice since this UK director had made his name with *Robbery* (1967), *Bullitt* (1968) and *The Hot Rock* (1972), all of them action thrillers — although at least the last of these, based on the Donald Westlake novel, had been a comedy as well as a crime movie.

Nevertheless, *For Pete's Sake* was performed adequately, and it is certainly entertaining enough, being co-written by Stanley Shapiro, who had acted in the same capacity for *Pillow Talk* (1959) for Doris Day and Rock Hudson years earlier. But, seeming dated even on its release (though still playing well on television, where its real home is), this is unquestionably a routine outing – a cheap-feeling, wet-afternoon, escape-from-the-rain sort of movie. Streisand vehicles have always been supposed to be special events.

This minor cloud was to have a major silver lining. *For Pete's Sake* was memorable to Barbra 'for Peters' sake'. It was while working on this movie that she met the ruggedly handsome Beverly Hills hairdresser Jon Peters, and she seems to have fallen instantly in love. Peters, of Italian-Cherokee origin, was then 28, a few years younger than Streisand, and was still married to actress Lesley Ann Warren. He created the rather odd-looking short-hair wig Streisand wears in the movie. Soon he became a more significant and intimate part of both her private and business life. In 1976 Peters took

ABOVE: A hair raising experience: For Pete's Sake.

over as her manager from Marty Erlichman, who had performed the service ever since 1961. Peters went on to produce *A Star Is Born* (1976) and *The Main Event* (1979), both with Streisand starring, and, notably, *Eyes of Laura Mars* (1978), which starred Faye Dunaway and Tommy Lee Jones.

However, the Barbra-Jon relationship would in due course peter out in the early 1980s during the 18 months she spent in Europe making *Yentl* (1983). Barbra was the one who decided to end it, symbolizing the deed by buying his Malibu land from him. Marty Erlichman, who in the interim produced such films as *Coma* (1978) and *Breathless* (1983), would return to the job of being Streisand's manager in 1988. Meanwhile Peters went on to become one of Hollywood's most powerful players, responsible for producing, along with his partner Peter Gruber – they formed the Gruber-Peters company in 1982 – *The Color Purple* (1985), *Rain Man* (1988) and Warner's biggest-ever hit, *Batman* (1989). For a time the two ran Columbia Pictures after it was taken over by Sony in 1989.

It seems that the number one female star was not finding the material she needed, though it is hard to know quite why this should be: Streisand was at the very top of the Hollywood tree, and writers must have been falling over themselves to pen scripts especially for her. Of course, there is always a dearth of good scripts, and just by happenstance there did not seem to be any brilliant ones tailored for Barbra's special needs around at the time. 'I wish some of the film scripts that were written for Bette Davis could be written for me today,' she remarked.

And so it was that in 1975, finding nothing new she fancied, Streisand opted for a sequel to her 1968 hit *Funny Girl,* called rather unimaginatively *Funny Lady* (1975). This reprised, less successfully, her role as Fanny Brice. 'These two films are my bookends,' she said: 'My Fanny Brice syndrome!'

The new movie, which reunited her with producer Ray Stark and the director of *The Owl and the Pussycat,* Herbert Ross,

LEFT: 'I Found A Million Dollar Baby', from Funny Lady.

was a respectable performer at the box office and is generally agreed to be good but not on a par with the original, although once again the songs came to the rescue of a so-so project, giving it a measure of class. Indeed, the new tunes – from Fred Ebb and John Kander (the songwriters of *Cabaret*) – are outstanding, particularly the jaunty 'How Lucky Can You Get' and the rousing 'Let's Hear It For Me'. Along with 1930s standards like 'So Long Honey Lamb', 'It's Only A Paper Moon', 'If I Love Again', 'More Than You Know' and 'Am I Blue', the *Funny Lady* songs added up to a delightful musical package that gave her another deserved hit album. 'How Lucky' and the score were nominated for Oscars, as were the cinematography and sound, but on the night the members of the Academy gave the film the thumbs down. Even so, the $8.5 million movie took $19 million at the US box office – not bad at a time when musicals were looking so shaky.

Returning yet again to the musicals vein, Streisand decided to make the third film version of *A Star Is Born* (1976), dangerously inviting comparison with her illustrious predecessor Judy Garland, who had starred with James Mason in George Cukor's warmly regarded second version in 1954 (and on whose television show, we recall, Streisand had appeared so memorably back in the 1960s). Garland and Mason had given their most luminous performances in that picture, with its keynote Harold Arlen-George Gershwin songs, like 'The Man That Got Away'; while the 1937 version, starring Fredric March and Janet Gaynor, is also considered one of cinema's highspots. No doubt this weight of cinema history helped to incur the wrath of some critics and perhaps explains why Streisand's movie got such an unfairly rough critical reception on release, though more likely

---

'These two films are my bookends, my Fanny Brice syndrome!'
ON *FUNNY GIRL* AND *FUNNY LADY*

---

some people just thought Streisand (credited on screen for two songs and 'musical concepts') had become too big for her boots and that it was time she was cut down to size. The movie was produced by Jon Peters, who had by now established himself as an important new power in the film-making business.

In the Streisand version the classic 1930s story of showbiz's ups and downs is relocated from the movie world to the

pop music environment of the 1970s. The shift of venue can be deemed a success, and, apart from its shared theme, the film is really totally unlike its two predecessors, forming an attractive, highly professional, often throbbingly vibrant package that is definitely no mere remake. The movie and its lovely song 'Evergreen' (for which Streisand won an Oscar as co-composer with Paul Williams) turned out to be big hits, but the making was by all reports a nightmare. Streisand allegedly argued vehemently with co-star Kris Kristofferson and director Frank Pierson (both of whom complained publicly about her interference), and fell out with musical director Paul Williams. These stories scarcely helped the Streisand image.

For the movie Barbra also co-wrote the song 'Lost Inside Of You' with Leon Russell. Paul Williams and Kenny Asher contributed the majority of the tunes, including 'Watch Closely Now', 'Spanish Lies', 'Hellacious Acres', 'With One More Look At You' and 'Woman In The Moon'.

Though the critics generally scoffed at *A Star Is Born,* dubbing it, for example, 'A Bore Is Starred' and 'A Star Is Still-Born', Streisand's fans were outraged at

LEFT: The third version of A Star Is Born: *wags called it 'A Bore Is Starred'.*

the attacks on a well-made, entertaining old-fashioned star vehicle and totally satisfied by the story, film-making and Streisand's singing and performance. Particularly they were pleased by the film's exciting finale: ten minutes of concert footage of the star shot in Phoenix, Arizona. Certainly Streisand had enough fans willing to line up at the box office to turn *A Star Is Born* into a money-spinner. At the end of the day the movie proved to be one of her best and most satisfying star vehicles and probably her biggest artistic success. She must have felt that all the hassles, heartache and hard work had been worthwhile.

This was a difficult time for Barbra professionally, as she dithered about her next picture. Among the projects she considered was a remake of *Annie Get Your Gun* (1950) and a film with Sean Connery. Apparently when she asked him if he would be directed by her, he replied: 'Good God no, why should I? I've made more pictures than you. Would you be directed by me?'

So three years went by after the making of *A Star is Born* until finally, in October 1978, Jon Peters oversaw the filming of a boxing comedy called *The Main Event* (1979), with Streisand

as co-executive producer. This project reunited her with her friend, former lover and former co-star Ryan O'Neal. The script, originally called *Knockout*, had been planned for Diana Ross and James Caan, but it was sent to O'Neal when Caan bowed out. Around this time boxing fan Peters got to see it and

LEFT: The Main Event *in 1979 was the rematch of Barbra and Ryan O'Neal, but it proved no knockout.*

thoroughly admired it, and he talked Barbra into taking the project on. At first she was dubious about its virtues, but she wanted to do an easy-going comedy after all the traumas of *A Star is Born* and she believed in Peters' gut reactions about what constituted a money-making hit. Moreover, boxing pictures were very much in vogue in Hollywood at the time, after the smash success of Sylvester Stallone's *Rocky* (1976), which had taken everyone by surprise. O'Neal – who had been Hollywood's golden boy when he and Barbra were working on *What's Up, Doc?* – was especially pleased to do the film with the high-profile Streisand, since his career had started to stall after *The Driver* (1978) and *Oliver's Story* (1978) had done disappointing box-office business. In fact, even apart from his considerable comedy skills, O'Neal was ideally cast, as he was in top physical shape and once upon a time had been a boxer. With O'Neal on board, wits dubbed the forthcoming film *Glove Story* . . . and perhaps it is a pity that Peters and Streisand did not choose this title rather than the one they eventually decided upon! *The Main Event,* as a title, is not much of an improvement on the original *Knockout.*

ABOVE: Barbra joins the battle of the sexes for what turned out to be a non-event.

Though the film was an obvious attempt to recapture the magic of *What's Up, Doc?,* lightning resolutely refused to strike twice, and Streisand's reunion with O'Neal turned out to be a still-born non-event. O'Neal played the clapped-out fighter Eddie 'The Kid' Scanlon, who is inherited by broke perfume mogul Streisand. She has been cheated by her accountant, and now sets out to turn O'Neal into a winner again so she can recoup some of her fortune. There was nothing wrong with the screwball-style premise, casting or director (comedy expert Howard Zieff, who had just had a hit with 1978's *House Calls*) but, after the highs of *A Star Is Born,* the Streisand-Peters duo experienced a critical panning in the always risky field of movie comedy.

Nevertheless, despite deservedly rotten reviews, the public stayed with the Streisand-O'Neal combination, and *The Main Event* did creditable box-office business, raking in $26 million. As the budget had been a low $7 million, this monetary success must have provided much spiritual consolation for Streisand and Peters – but *The Main Event* was not at all the kind of film Barbra needed to enhance her career.

At the same time, the professional problem of a lacklustre movie was combined with a personal one: Peters reputedly became jealous of the time Barbra spent working with her former lover – ironic, because it was Peters who had persuaded Barbra to do the movie with O'Neal in the first place. Peters and O'Neal were reported as having taken part in a serious boxing match together before the filming began, but whether this was for sport or for real remains a matter of gossip. Either way, it probably helped let off some steam.

On the subject of *The Main Event* major US critic John Simon delivered what could be described as a blow below the belt: 'This summer may go down in history as the summer of horror movies, but none of these can match Barbra Streisand and her latest offering.' *Motion Picture Guide* added bitchily: 'It's a shame that the male lead was prettier than the female, but that's usually the case with Streisand.' *Variety* was little kinder:

'This summer may go down in history as the summer of horror movies, but none of these can match Barbra Streisand and her latest offering.'
JOHN SIMON ON **THE MAIN EVENT**

'Instead of a comic knockout this is more of a cream puff.' There was a small clutch of accompanying songs, some of which were pretty dreary, though Streisand's spunky rendition of the medley disc marrying the two best songs, 'The Main Event' and 'Fight', both by

Paul Jabara and Bruce Roberts, provided her with a hit that reached Number Three in the US charts.

Jabara, meanwhile, talked Barbra into recording his new song 'No More Tears (Enough is Enough)', with the disco queen Donna Summer for her *Wet* album. It turned out to be one of Barbra's biggest singles, hitting Number One in the USA at the end of 1979 – and greatly impressing her 12-year-old son Jason.

While the director of *The Main Event,* Howard Zieff, ironically went straight on to make his biggest hit, *Private Benjamin* (1980) with Goldie Hawn, things did not immediately improve for Barbra. In 1981, just voted American National Theater Owners Female Star of the Decade, Streisand stepped, apparently for the first time, into a project she had not originated, and she probably soon regretted it. This time Leonard Goldberg and Jerry Weintraub (rather than Jon Peters) were to be the producers; the little-known director was the Belgian-born Jean-Claude Tramont, who had experience of only one previous movie, which he had made in France. This was his first US movie.

All Night Long (1981) started as a low-budget picture (at just $3.5 million) with Lisa Eichhorn – star of *Yanks* (1979) and *Cutter's Way* (1981; also known as *Cutter and Bone*) – as a wacky young married woman who is the object of the attentions of a married middle-aged businessman (Gene Hackman). He is a California pharmacy boss who decides to chuck in the rat race and his wife (Diane Ladd) and family for a final fling at true love and real happiness. The girl, who is married to Hackman's cousin (Kevin Dobson), is also having a fling with Hackman's son (Dennis Quaid). Despite these somewhat bizarre and contrived plot complications, essentially we've heard it all before, but W.D. Richter's oddball script has a genuine go at making it fresh and witty, and this – plus the deal of a lifetime – must have been what attracted Barbra's eye.

Three and a half weeks after the apparently troubled film was in production, Streisand unexpectedly replaced Eichhorn, dismissed by the director Tramont on the grounds that, apparently, she was just not funny ('The part was too much of a stretch for Lisa,' he said). If the sacking caused a sensation in Hollywood, even more so did the deal that was carved out. When Streisand stepped in she took second billing for what is obviously a co-starring (and rewritten) part, but, in an extraordinary deal, took a then astonishing $4 million and 15 per cent of the picture's gross earnings for just five weeks' work! Eichhorn's deal had been for $250,000, which she was able to keep.

The mystery surrounding all this seems to lead back to a single phone call made by Tramont's wife Sue Mengers, who by chance was also Streisand's agent. Mengers made the call in response to her husband's film-making difficulties. Whatever the rights and wrongs of the situation, the main loser was Eichhorn, as there is no doubt that her promising career was damaged by this dismissal – though in truth everybody came out of the film smelling of manure. Tramont has never made another Hollywood picture; Hackman's career went into a shaky phase; and Mengers ceased to be Streisand's agent.

The film did garner respectable reviews, though it must have been frustrating to Streisand that it was Hackman who attracted all the critical attention and credit. Most critics agreed that Barbra was basically miscast and wasted – though not entirely ineffectual – in a low-key supporting performance. Then, if this were not bad enough news for her, there was further frustration when the movie, with its weird Streisand-Hackman star pairing, didn't catch on with the public.

With two duds in the five years since *A Star Is Born,* the Streisand movie career was in the doldrums. There is little doubt that it was this dire situation which spurred her to what in the event was a remarkable comeback. She took over the entire control of her destiny. To fail now, with a challenge so great, would have been impossible for 'the greatest star'.

DIRECTOR SUPERSTAR

'I was frightened to direct. I didn't know if I could do it. But I was nearing 40 years old and thinking that I must take more risks as an artist and as a person. I had this vision of becoming this old lady and talking about this movie I should have made.'

FACING PAGE: *Ready for* Yentl.

One day while in the middle of filming on location for *The Main Event*,
Streisand turned to Jon Peters and proclaimed 'I hate this movie. I'm going to
do *Yentl.*' So it was that, five years of
intensive pre-production work later, in
1982 she finally set out to realize her
deeply held dream. She was embarking
on the strongest possible comeback: as
director, co-writer, co-producer and star
of the Jewish musical *Yentl,* an adaptation
of the Isaac Bashevis Singer short story
'Yentl the Yeshiva Boy'. It was to cost

*BELOW: 'The story is
Yentl's redemption from
self-hatred': Streisand.*

the troubled MGM/United Artists studio
a worryingly high $18 million but, as
events were to prove, fears over the
costs were unwarranted, as *Yentl* performed strongly, taking over $20 million
at the US box office alone. This long-
cherished Streisand project — she had
bought the film rights to the Singer work
14 years earlier — is obviously a personal
vision. This quality is up there on the
screen, and is perhaps the movie's most
attractive feature.

Streisand plays a turn-of-the-century
young Polish woman called Yentl who
poses as a boy to learn the Torah, since
in 1904 girls are not permitted to make
such studies. This understandably confuses
both Streisand's co-star Amy Irving,
whom she 'marries' in the story, and her
male fellow student Mandy Patinkin,
with whom she falls in love. A clause of
Hasidic law says Patinkin cannot marry
his fiancée Irving, since his brother has
committed suicide, so it is he who is
responsible for persuading the couple to
get spliced, telling Streisand this will
bring him closer to Irving. Most people
might soon after this have started to sus-
pect something about Streisand's gender
(even though she is surprisingly effective
and convincing as a male youth), but

Patinkin and Irving remain blissfully unaware of the situation.

To make clear her serious intentions in the area of sexual politics, Streisand ensured the advertising line on the posters read: 'In a time when the world

> *'I hate this movie [THE MAIN EVENT]. I'm going to do YENTL.'*

of study belonged only to men, there lived a girl who dared to ask "why?"' As co-writer (with Jack Rosenthal), she amusingly brought out the feminist message of the Shakespeare-style gender-bending story without banging on about it, and as actress she turned in a skilful, charismatic performance.

The long, arduous location shoot took place in Czechoslovakia, in difficult physical conditions, around a small town called Roztyly, some distance from Prague. The location filming started in July 1982 and finished in October. Streisand was later satisfied when MGM/United Artists, who had a contractual right to vet the movie's final cut, did not interfere with her vision, and

Yentl opened in 1983 in time for the much-hoped-for Oscar nominations.

Just before production started, Streisand had formed her own production company, Barwood Films. Pleasingly, *Yentl* was its first movie.

The Golden Globe evening in January 1984 was a sensation for Streisand and *Yentl*. She was visibly astonished to be given the Best Director award, thereby becoming the first woman director to

ABOVE: A wave of success: on location in Czechoslovakia for Yentl.

win a Golden Globe. 'Directing was for me a total experience. It calls upon everything you've ever seen or felt or known or heard. It was really the highlight of my . . . professional life,' she told the gathered VIPs.

The Golden Globes are supposed to be indications of how the Oscars will go – although, ominously, Streisand did not win the Directors' Guild of America Award. Yet in February 1984 she was upset when the Oscar nominations were announced and there were no major

'Directing was for me a total experience. It calls upon everything you've ever seen or felt or known or heard. It was really the highlight of my . . . professional life.'

nominations for *Yentl*. Instead there were three music nominations, one for art direction and another for Amy Irving as Best Supporting Actress.

Naturally, for *Yentl* once again Streisand took care that a major factor in the film was the music though, since musicals were out of fashion, the production was advertised as not a musical but 'A Film with Music'. The attractive, yearning score by Michel Legrand scooped an Oscar, which proved to be the film's sole Academy Award victory. Legrand was also responsible for the dozen appealing tunes (with lyrics supplied by old colleagues Alan Bergman and Marilyn Bergman), producing a brace of hits – 'Papa, Can You Hear Me?' and 'The Way He Makes Me Feel' – both of which were Oscar-nominated. Other songs to remember include 'A Piece Of

BELOW: 'Everything Barbra has done before Yentl has been a rehearsal': Amy Irving (right).

Sky', 'No Matter What Happens', 'This Is One Of Those Moments', 'Tomorrow Night', 'Where Is It Written', 'No Wonder' and 'Will Someone Ever Look at Me That Way?' These attractive songs are used effectively to link the narrative and vocalize interior feelings, in much the same way that Shakespeare used soliloquies.

Critics argued over the film's artistic merits, particularly in terms of the direction, writing and music, which bore the brunt of any attacks, but technically it is indisputably a fine piece of work and therefore ultimately a great credit to its *auteur,* Streisand. *Yentl* is a beautifully acted, eye-catchingly handsome film. Art director Roy Walker, although he did not win the Oscar, at least had the satisfaction of winning a nomination for his work; but UK cinematographer David Watkin was robbed when he was not even nominated for his evocative, Old Dutch Master-style Technicolor images.

Naturally the critics had their knives out for the first-time director. *Motion Picture Guide* said 'Singer's beautiful short story is turned into a musical ego trip. A potentially interesting drama quickly turns into Streisand's homage to her own talents.'

Streisand's relationship with Jon Peters had been breaking up during the 18 months of European work on *Yentl.* Barbra looked around for a new beau, and one soon popped up to introduce himself to her — at a 1983 Christmas party. Tall, handsome Richard Baskin, heir to the Baskin-Robbins ice-cream company, was a movie musical director who had worked with Robert Altman on *Buffalo Bill and the Indians* (1976) and *Nashville* (1975), for which he wrote several of the country songs. Barbra enlisted him as one of the producers on her *Emotion* album, released in October 1984. Though not one of her best or most successful albums, this went platinum. One of the singles from it, 'Left In The Dark', became the basis for Streisand's debut music video.

Fired by the success of *Yentl,* Streisand searched throughout the 1980s for a similar challenge, rekindling in herself the desire she had always felt to extend her range and play what she felt were some of the great roles she could match up to, like Medea and Hedda Gabler. Among the other possible irons in her fire were the long-vaunted film of the Andrew Lloyd Webber musical *Evita;* an art film with Ingmar Bergman (who had directed, none too successfully, Elliott Gould in *The Touch* in 1971); a movie with Jane Fonda to be called *The Triangle Fire;* and a screwball comedy pairing her with Goldie Hawn. All of these were tantalizing projects, and the range of material on offer was exceptionally wide, but alas they were all to come to naught.

With the frustrations of her movie ambitions unresolved, she concentrated instead on her music career, and came up with a winner. After the relative failure of her previous pop album *Emotion*, she decided to revisit her show-tune roots. The result, a triumph of total public and critical acclaim, was *The Broadway Album* (1985), produced with the help of Paul Jabara (her *Main Event* associate), another old colleague, Peter Matz, and Stephen Sondheim, who even reworked some of his classic show tunes for her. 'It turned out to be so exhilarating, there were moments when I was screaming with joy,' said Barbra. *The Broadway Album* was released in November, and before Christmas had shot to Number One. It unexpectedly became her bestselling album, winning Barbra her eighth Grammy. It was also a personal victory: her record company had earlier expressed negative views about the project.

The film of Tom Topor's fine Broadway play *Nuts* had been planned way back in 1981 with Mark Rydell – of *The Rose* (1979) and *On Golden Pond* (1981), for which he was Oscar-nominated – as director. First Bette Midler (Oscar-nominated for *The Rose*) and then later Debra Winger – riding high after her Oscar nominations for *An Officer and a Gentleman* (1982) and *Terms of Endearment* (1983) – were to star. *Nuts* boasts one of those rare scripts – with a strong central woman's role and a supremely crafted, intelligent story full of meaning and resonance – that Hollywood's top actresses are willing to fight over. Unfortunately, both Midler's career and Rydell's, then Winger's, took a dip at the wrong moment for them. In Hollywood you are only as good as your last movie, and Midler had made the foolishly titled *Jinxed* (1982), Winger had made *Mike's Murder* (1983) and Rydell had made *The River* (1984) – all three of which had been high-profile flops. The careers of the two actresses and the director recovered in due course, as history tells us, but not in time for them to get back aboard *Nuts*.

Once Streisand, smelling of roses from *Yentl*, became involved in the project, a small film suddenly escalated to a big-budget number (around $21.5 million, which jumped to an eventual $27.5 million) — as had now become a familiar pattern in her career. She herself was commanding $5 million as star and $500,000 more as producer, though she waived her payment as co-writer.

By 1985, though, Universal had become disenchanted with the project. It was revived at Warners, but soon after that Rydell left the production, apparently taking his fee with him. Barbra then asked for Martin Ritt to take over as director, as she had long admired his liberal-thinking work on high-prestige, top-quality, Oscar-bound films like *Hud* (1963), *Conrack* (1974), *The Front* (1976) and *Norma Rae* (1979). At their first meeting he reportedly said: 'I'd like to do this movie. There's only one thing: I don't know if you could play the part.' 'Good, you're the one,' she is said to have replied.

After Dustin Hoffman left the film, shooting began with Richard Dreyfuss in the main co-starring role, as Streisand's lawyer defending her high-class-hooker, Claudia Draper. Draper may or may not be psychotic, and Dreyfuss tries to prevent her being locked up for her own

good as insane after she has killed one of her clients (Leslie Nielsen), apparently in self-defence. Dreyfuss opposes the hooker's parents wishes to prove she is sane enough to be tried for the killing. Karl Malden played her stepfather, with Maureen Stapleton as her mother, Eli Wallach as the psychiatrist, James Whitmore as the judge and Robert Webber as the prosecuting attorney.

After all the cast changes and delays. *Nuts* could hardly have been better — different, maybe, but not better. Barbra related closely to the story of being

ABOVE: A word to the wise: Richard Dreyfuss as Streisand's lawyer defending her in Nuts.

abused as a child, though in her case the stepfather's abuse had been emotional rather than physical or sexual. Typically, she took the role very seriously, visiting psychoanalysts, psychiatric hospitals and mentally disturbed women patients.

BELOW: Courting trouble: Streisand acts on the edge in Nuts.

The film finally got under way in October 1986, a full five years after it

had first been announced to the public. Barbra produced, wrote the score, had a hand in the script and, with the contractual right to do the final cut, re-edited Ritt's version of the picture. In the print as released in 1987, despite arguable miscasting and a director who seemed never fully to have believed she was ideal for the part, Streisand produces a

heartrending performance that the majority of viewers can really believe in and be moved by. Indeed, most people would agree that all the acting and the film itself are commendable; some would be even more complimentary than that. If the 44-year-old movie queen Barbra was not perhaps entirely right for the part, her performance was certainly able to sway sympathetic viewers into believing that she was. Nevertheless, as always when Streisand performs in a dramatic role, she received mixed reviews among some generous notices. This mixture was reflected in the public's reception of the film.

Among the reviews, Kenneth Turan, writing in *Premiere,* was particularly cutting: 'Streisand tries hard to act on the edge, but achieves only the kind of whiny, irritating petulance a Beverly Hills matron might exhibit if someone grabbed her parking space. It's so close to the woe-is-me-do-I-have-troubles Streisand persona we've seen in just about every one of her films that the idea of her being a real character barely enters our minds.' *Motion Picture Guide* still hammered away relentlessly at Streisand's appearance: 'Did Streisand cast Webber, Stapleton and Malden, who sport three of the biggest schnozzes in the business, to make her own nose look smaller, like the nightclub owner who hires midget waiters to make the drinks look bigger?' No wonder Barbra is sensitive about her appearance! Nevertheless *Motion Picture Guide's* grudging final verdict was: 'She showed remarkable restraint . . . producer Streisand has wisely opted to surround star Streisand with a terrific complement of actors . . . As a story, it's thin. As cinema, it's static. There is enough in all the performances to make it a diversion, but little more.' Just the kind of damning with faint praise that kills a film at the box office. *Variety* said: 'A premise weighted down by portentous performances. While the film ignites sporadically, it succumbs to the burden of its own earnestness. Streisand is good but it's too much of a good thing.'

The shaky reviews, added to what could in the first place be perceived as a depressing subject matter, took their toll, and meant that, when the accounts were finally in, a picture that cost $27.5 million made only $14 million at the US box office.

Alarmingly for the future of her film career, people were saying that the golden Streisand allure was tarnished, that she had lost her magic box-office touch. As a consolation prize for *Nuts,* perhaps, around this time Barbra – whose relationship with Richard Baskin had resolved itself into the two being just good friends – was linked romantically to actor Don Johnson. She had first encountered him when he mispronounced her name as Strei-*zund* when announcing her as winner in the Best Female Pop Vocal category for *The Broadway Album* at the 1987 Grammy Award ceremony; the duo first met properly at a Colorado Christmas party on Boxing Day 1987. In February the following year, when Barbra was again voted Female Star of the Decade, she arrived to receive her award alongside Johnson and was touchingly greeted by her old friend Jon Peters. Afterwards she appeared in a cameo on Johnson's *Miami Vice* show and turned up at the movie premiere of his *Sweet Hearts Dance* (1988).

Later that year, though, Johnson rekindled his love for ex-wife Melanie Griffith – a shift of emotional allegiances that apparently stunned Barbra – and the former married couple re-wed in the spring of 1989.

So, unlucky in love, in 1989 Streisand tried to resume her movie career with renewed zest. Her path, though, proved to be littered with foiled plans. She was forced to suffer a couple of blows to the ego when Kathleen Turner was preferred to her for the female lead in *The War of the Roses* (1989) and Michelle Pfeiffer in *Frankie and Johnny* (1991). An intriguing plan for her to play the quintessential indomitable showbiz mother Rose opposite Madonna's Gypsy Rose Lee in a remake of Stephen Sondheim's Broadway musical *Gypsy* failed (eventually Bette Midler did it, in 1994) and so did her proposed biopic of Margaret Bourke-White (with Richard Gere as author Erskine Caldwell).

Instead, in 1991, she decided to go back to her troubled roots 50 years ago, and dig deep into the apparently still unhealed issues arising from her childhood. It was her friend Don Johnson who first got her to read Pat Conroy's novel *The Prince of Tides,* about a dysfunctional Southern family, initially hoping the couple might appear in a film version of it together. But then Robert Redford was first off the mark to buy the rights in the book; with Barbra interested as well, it looked on the cards that there would be an intriguing reunion of the two *The Way We Were* stars. However, Redford withdrew from the project for

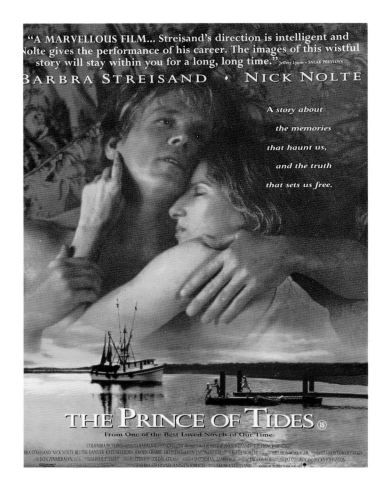

'artistic reasons' when Streisand wanted not only to act but also to direct.

After all the negotiations were over, Streisand did indeed direct herself, for the second time, in *The Prince of Tides* (1991), playing a psychiatrist opposite the

ABOVE: The tide of critical acclaim goes to Barbra's co-star Nick Nolte.

emotionally confused patient acted by Nick Nolte. His sister (Melinda Dillon) is disturbed, suicidal and catatonic, and Streisand must, with Nolte's help, find the key to the past that will set everybody's lives right in the present. In a very Freudian story, a disturbed childhood leading to an unhappy adulthood is at the heart of the movie. The Streisand character is herself part of a dysfunctional family, with a dreadful, selfish husband (Jeroen Krabbe) and an estranged son. The story sees the burgeoning of an unethical but healing romance between Streisand and unhappily married Nolte; the romance proves extremely moving, as Nolte reaches lovingly out to help Streisand's needy son.

The Prince of Tides gave Barbra the opportunity to work with her real-life son, Jason Gould, who touchingly took the part of her violin-playing fictional son. This shared work was important to both of them. It brought them closer together in an act of mutual understanding which reflected some of the healing themes of the film.

Although Streisand was a mite improbable as a psychiatrist – aside from anything else, the film often seems oddly obsessed with her beautiful hands, which bear astonishingly long fingernails – this beautifully crafted movie oozes care and love from every frame. It won much-deserved praise, especially for the truly outstanding performance by Nolte, who gained a Golden Globe as Best Actor.

Then, encouragingly, the film picked up seven Academy Award nominations: Best Film, Best Actor (Nolte), Best Supporting Actress (Kate Nelligan), Best Adapted Screenplay, Best Cinematography, Best Original Score and Best Art Direction. But, on the night, *The Silence of the Lambs* (1990) swept the Oscar board, leaving nothing at all for *The Prince of Tides.* Hardly surprisingly, this desperately disappointed Streisand, who herself had not even been nominated in the categories Best Actor or Best Director.

Though of course she won a Best Actress Oscar for her very first movie, *Funny Girl,* and was later nominated in the same category for her part in *The Way We Were,* Barbra has never been nominated as Best Director. This has prompted her to feel that she is being discriminated against – as a woman with a fierce reputation for toughness and meticulousness – by the voting members of the Academy of Motion Picture Arts and Sciences.

FILMOGRAPHY

BELOW: Dolly, you'll never go away again': Hello, Dolly!

1. *Funny Girl* (Columbia) 1968. Directed by William Wyler. Streisand as Fanny Brice, with Omar Sharif, Kay Medford, Anne Francis and Walter Pidgeon.

2. *Hello, Dolly!* (Twentieth Century-Fox) 1969. Directed by Gene Kelly. Streisand as Dolly Levi, with Walter Matthau and Michael Crawford.

3. *On a Clear Day You Can See Forever* (Paramount) 1970. Directed by Vincente Minnelli. Streisand as Daisy Gamble and Melinda Tentrees, with Yves Montand, Jack Nicholson, Bob Newhart and John Richardson.

4. *The Owl and the Pussycat* (Columbia) 1970. Directed by Herbert Ross. Streisand as Doris Wilgus, with George Segal, Robert Klein and Allen Garfield.

5. *What's Up, Doc?* (Warner) 1972. Directed by Peter Bogdanovich. Streisand as Judy Maxwell, with Ryan O'Neal, Madeline Kahn, Austin Pendleton and Kenneth Mars.

6. *Up the Sandbox* (First Artists) 1972. Directed by Irvin Kershner. Streisand as Margaret Reynolds, with David Selby, Ariane Heller and Paul Benedict.

7. *The Way We Were* (Columbia) 1973. Directed by Sydney Pollack. Streisand as Katie Morosky, with Robert Redford, Bradford Dillman, Patrick O'Neal and Lois Chiles.

8. *For Pete's Sake* (Columbia) 1974. Directed by Peter Yates. Streisand as Henrietta Robbins, with Michael

Sarrazin, Estelle Parsons, William Redfield and Molly Picon.

9. *Funny Lady* (Columbia) 1975. Directed by Herbert Ross. Streisand as Fanny Brice, with James Caan, Omar Sharif, Roddy McDowall and Carole Wells.

10. *A Star is Born* (Warner) 1976. Directed by Frank Pierson. Streisand as Esther Hoffman, with Kris Kristofferson, Paul Mazursky, Gary Busey and Joanne Linville.

11. *The Main Event* (Warner) 1979. Directed by Howard Zieff. Streisand as Hillary Kramer, with Ryan O'Neal, Paul Sand, James Gregory and Patti D'Arbanville.

12. *All Night Long* (Universal) 1981. Directed by Jean-Claude Tramont. Streisand as Cheryl Gibbons, with Gene Hackman, Dennis Quaid, Kevin Dobson and Diane Ladd.

13. *Yentl* (MGM/United Artists) 1983. Directed by Streisand. Streisand as Yentl/Yanshel, with Mandy Patinkin, Amy Irving, Nehemiah Persoff, Steven Hill and Miriam Margolyes.

14. *Nuts* (Warner) 1987. Directed by Martin Ritt. Streisand as Claudia Draper, with Richard Dreyfuss, Karl Malden, Maureen Stapleton, Eli Wallach, James Whitmore and Robert Webber.

15. *The Prince of Tides* (Columbia) 1991. Directed by Streisand. Streisand as Dr Susan Lowenstein, with Nick Nolte, Blythe Danner, Jason Gould, Jeroen Krabbe, Melinda Dillon and George Carlin.

ABOVE: Streisand as Margaret Reynolds in the 1972 film, Up the Sandbox.

STREISAND TODAY

---

*'I understand why the conservatives attack us.
They deem us a very dangerous crowd,
especially because of the kind of money some
of us can raise for the Democrats.'*

FACING PAGE: 'There seems to be a need for this diva thing.'

Fighting to be a star in the first place, fighting to perform songs her way, fighting to make the movies she wanted, fighting to survive in the glare of the media – Barbra has always been a fighter. No doubt that gave her the confidence to enter an even more risky arena – politics and campaigning. Streisand, brought up in poor, working-class Brooklyn, felt strongly about what she saw as the unfairness of the 1980s Reaganite society. In 1988 she supported the Democratic

---

'Few of us have responded with enough urgency to meet this crisis of catastrophic proportions, certainly not the last two presidents. . . I will never forgive my fellow actor Ronald Reagan for the genocidal denial of the illness's existence, for his refusal to even utter the word AIDS for seven years and for blocking adequate funding for research and education which could have saved hundreds of thousands of lives.'

ON AIDS

---

presidential candidate Michael Dukakis not just privately but publicly, with events like her headlining appearance at a Los Angeles fund-raising concert. US liberals, particularly those in Hollywood, were very excited at this time after the long (and what they saw as repressive and uncaring) Republican era of Ronald Reagan, and hopeful that the 1990s, like the 1960s era heralded by the arrival of President Kennedy, would see, as it were, a new Camelot. But Dukakis, battling against the largely right-wing media, proved a surprisingly lacklustre candidate and the Republican George Bush was elected.

The liberals had to wait another four years for their turn at a new society, but this time they were all resolved to try harder – and that included an increasingly politicized and confident Barbra. This time there was no mistake. When Bill Clinton was elected president Barbra performed as top of the bill at his inaugural gala in Landover, Maryland, on January 19, 1993. She sang 'Evergreen' and 'Children Will Listen', commenting: 'We cannot abuse children, either by word or deed. What is done to them, they will do to society.' Afterwards the president-elect was pictured on stage hugging her gleefully. In this emotional moment of recent US history, it seemed that the dispossessed – women, blacks, gays – had taken over the White House.

Meanwhile Barbra was becoming more involved in various charitable works. At last she took the plunge into the area of AIDS and gay campaigning, much to the joy of her legions of gay fans, many of whom had hitherto criticized her for not becoming publicly involved in this life-or-death issue, in the way that Elizabeth Taylor had. In 1992 Streisand became a director of Hollywood Supports, and gave $350,000 to help AIDS charities through her Streisand Foundation. She sang at the Commitment to Life benefit show in Los Angeles on September 18, 1992, and told the audience in a surprisingly no-holds-barred statement: 'Few of us have responded with enough urgency to meet this crisis of catastrophic proportions, certainly not the last two presidents . . . I will never forgive my fellow actor Ronald Reagan for the genocidal denial of the illness's existence, for his refusal to even utter the word AIDS for seven years and for blocking adequate funding for research and education which could have saved hundreds of thousands of

ABOVE: A big hand for the little lady.

lives.' She added that the radical right at that year's Republican Convention 'branded the concerns of women, gays, minorities and Democrats as Un-American. How dare they call us Un-American? When Pat Buchanan thundered "We stand with George Bush against the amoral idea that gay and

lesbian couples should have the same standing in law as married men and women" I wondered who is Pat Buchanan to pronounce anyone's love invalid!'

In the firing line for backing gay rights, supposed political ambitions (one paper dubbed her 'Senator Yentl') – which she has hotly denied – and for implying support of a boycott of Colorado (which had voted to rescind laws to protect gays' jobs and homes), she was soon in a further media glare. The press reported that the 51-year-old Barbra was dating the 23-year-old tennis player Andre Agassi, with whom she was seen at the US Open Tennis Tournament at New York's Forest Hills in September 1992 and the following summer at Wimbledon. The two apparently met after Agassi had contacted her to tell her how *The Prince of Tides* had affected him. The press need not have worried too much: the relationship was short-lived. But Barbra's emotional life apparently remains a matter of great media concern. In 1995 it was reported that she was seeing the actor Jon Voight, though this too seems to have been a brief encounter.

Her professional career, though, moved on apace. In December 1992 her continuing superstar status was confirmed

LEFT: Candid camera: Barbra enjoys a night out.

when she signed a new record and film contract with Sony for a staggering $60 million. Auspiciously, *Back to Broadway,* the sequel to the immensely successful *The Broadway Album,* was the first album under the new contract – it shot straight to the top of the charts, despite less good reviews than its predecessor.

Further to the joy of her fans, Barbra began once more to make concert appearances. Given the scale of her current work contract, it seemed odd that reportedly she went on tour because she was short of ready cash and burdened with heavy spending commitments, most of her money being tied up in investments which were not performing well. Around this time, unable to sell her Malibu real estate, she gave it to the Santa Monica Mountains Conservancy in return for a tax deal.

The concerts kicked off with a series of knockout performances in front of rapturous audiences of 15,000 people at the MGM Grand Garden in Las Vegas, starting on New Year's Eve 1993. She opened the show with *Sunset Boulevard's* 'As If We Never Said Goodbye' and continued with Stephen Sondheim's 'I'm Still Here' (Sondheim let her change the words, adding 'I kept my nose to spite

my face'). The shows were a huge money-spinner, with tickets costing up to $1000; the concerts are said to have grossed $13 million.

In March she announced her intention to tour for the first time since 1966. The tour included a huge triumph at London's Wembley Arena in April 1994. This thrilled her UK fans, since it was

LEFT: Streisand changed the words to Sondheim's 'I'm Still Here', adding 'I kept my nose to spite my face.'

her first appearance in their country since *Funny Girl,* 28 years before. The UK press were hostile, attacking the anomaly of the high ticket prices charged by a star who had publicly declared herself socially conscious (though Streisand ensured that some tickets were donated to charity), then attacking the show itself. Barbra battled stage fright with the help of an autocue and heavily scripted 'ad libs', incurring the contempt of some of the critics but entrancing the sell-out crowds, who created a new record in speed of ticket sales. Prince Charles attended one of the concerts — some of the charity

LEFT: *Serious Streisand: Barbra makes a spectacle of herself.*

'We did have a fight about how boring life would be if we were all the same. To me a perfect world would be a place in which we appreciate each other's differences. We're equal but not the same.'

---

tickets had gone to his own foundation. They had met 20 years earlier, and backstage afterwards he told her: 'You look pretty good after all these years.' She replied: 'You look pretty good yourself.'

Streisand next headed for Italy, then back to the United States for a tour that started in Washington, highlighted at New York's Madison Square Garden in

June and concluded in Anaheim's Arrowhead Pond. Happily there is a permanent record of all this excitement, since the shows were taped as a television special.

In 1996 she finally embarked on a new movie after a gap of five years. It was to have been the long-awaited film version of Larry Kramer's 1980s play *The Normal Heart,* with Barbra as producer, director and star. She first optioned this love story set against the AIDS epidemic back in 1986. During 1995 she spent a lot of time on the script with the author

— now himself afflicted by AIDS — and struggling to find finance for the project. She and Kramer seem to have enjoyed arguing over the script. 'We did have a fight about how boring life would be if we were all the same,' said Barbra. 'To me a perfect world would be a place in which we appreciate each other's differences. We're equal but not the same.'

'I think I'm always drawn into films about the mystery of appearances.'

But instead Barbra made a film with Jeff Bridges, *The Mirror Has Two Faces,* a romantic comedy about a frumpy professor who makes herself look glamorous to spark up her platonic marriage to a Columbia University maths teacher. Naturally Barbra plays the part of the transformed professor. 'I think I'm always drawn into films about the mystery of appearances,' she has said. '*The Mirror Has Two Faces* is a really charming love story. But it has serious overtones about vanity and beauty, the external versus the internal.' In total contrast to *The Normal Heart,* such upmarket romantic comedy material seems tailor-made for Barbra.

These two films seem to reflect the two faces of Streisand — the caring, socially aware human being and the old-time, escapist star. Fortunately there is room for both women in the world.

LEFT; Barbra in glamorous form at one of Hollywood's fabulous gala evenings in aid of charity.

RECORDING STAR

'I don't feel like a legend. I feel like a work in progress.'
ON RECEIVING THE GRAMMY LIFETIME ACHIEVEMENT AWARD

FACING PAGE: Ready for my close-up.

At the 1994 Grammy Awards ceremony, Barbra Streisand received a Special Lifetime Achievement Award. This was in recognition of the fact that for well over 30 years she had been one of the world's top musical entertainers. Streisand, who boasts one of the world's great popular voices – with a two-octave range – has notched up 50 albums so far, selling well over 100 million discs.

Her tally of albums is inflated by a proportion of minor works, including several 'greatest hits' collections and contributions to multi-artiste soundtracks. It is noticeable and surprising, given their quality and the publicity surrounding them, that the sales of the movie soundtrack albums are less spectacular than those of other ventures, even when the list contains major work like the *Funny Girl, Hello, Dolly!* and *Funny Lady* albums. In recent years, the success of the two *Broadway* albums has been significant, since Barbra has always been less comfortable and less exciting as a pop star than as the queen of the show tunes – the public seems to agree. But who would have thought that album collections of old show tunes would more than hold their own in a pop-dominated market? Streisand did. *The Broadway Album* became her all-time solo bestseller while *Back to Broadway* surprised the music business by hitting the Number One slot in the first week of its release, the first of her albums ever to do that.

Also significant is the success of the nostalgic four-album combined set *Just for the Record* in 1991, whose high cost did not put off the fans – and nor did the fact that it was her next release after *A Collection: Greatest Hits and More,* likewise an anthology album.

Though the recipient of eight Grammy Awards for her singing so far, Streisand won her last Grammy to date (for *The Broadway Album*) as long ago as 1985; she was nominated again in 1993

BELOW: Side by side with Sondheim's songs: Streisand scoops her eighth Grammy.

Barbra Streisand   *The Broadway Album*

for *Back to Broadway*. Her most recent release has been 1994's *Barbra: The Concert Album,* another ramble down memory lane. The fans are crying out for a collection of new songs.

Barbra's first contributions to an album can be heard on the 1962 Broadway cast recording of *I Can Get It for You Wholesale,* on which she sings four numbers, including her funny standout solo number 'Miss Marmelstein'. *Variety* opined: 'The material showstopper, and a lot of the credit should be given to Barbra Streisand's performance, is "Miss Marmelstein".' Next she gave six numbers to the 25th-anniversary recording of the musical revue *Pins and Needles*, with music and lyrics by Harold Rome (as for *I Can Get It for You Wholesale*). 'All hands are delightful,' said *Variety*.

Barbra's recording career took a major leap forward after she made her album debut proper with *The Barbra Streisand Album,* released in February 1963 under her lucrative deal with Columbia. Her renditions of the torch songs 'Cry Me A River' and 'Soon It's Gonna Rain' are the standouts, though exuberant comic numbers like 'Who's Afraid Of The Big Bad Wolf?' remain appealing for novelty value alone. *The Barbra Streisand Album* became a gold record, reaching Number Eight in *Billboard's* Top 200, and it scooped three Grammy Awards: Best Album of the Year, Best Female Vocals and Best Album Cover. *Variety* said: 'Streisand's vocal dramatics pull her first LP into the best-selling class and

---

'Streisand's vocal dramatics pull her first LP into the best-selling class and establish her as the foremost young singer on discs.'
VARIETY

---

establish her as the foremost young singer on discs.'

Within 18 months she followed it with *The Second Barbra Streisand Album,* released in August 1963. Again the ballads are the standouts, particularly her rendition of 'Who Will Buy?' from *Oliver!* and her single releases, 'My Coloring Book' and 'When The Sun Comes Out Again'. Five of the tracks were by vintage composer Harold Arlen.

The Second Barbra Streisand Album

Any Place I Hang
My Hat Is Home
Right as the Rain
Down With Love
Who Will Buy?
When the Sun Comes Out
Gotta Move
My Coloring Book
I Don't Care Much
Lover, Come Back to Me
I Stayed Too Long
at the Fair
Like a Straw in the Wind
*Arranged and Conducted
by Peter Matz*

ABOVE: The Second
Barbra Streisand
Album *goes gold and
reaches Number Two in
the US LP chart.*

The Second Barbra Streisand Album likewise became a gold album, doing even better than before, this time reaching Number Two in the *Billboard* Top 200. *Variety* said: 'Arlen's moody melodies suit her perfectly and she kicks off each one with a potent delivery.' *Barbra Streisand: The Third Album* was released quickly afterwards, in February 1963. It too went gold, though this time reaching only Number Five in the charts. Perhaps a shade less exciting than its predecessors, *The Third Album* boasts fine renditions of the standards 'Bewitched, Bothered And Bewildered', 'My Melancholy Baby' and 'It Had To Be You', as well as a lovely new song, 'Draw Me A Circle'.

Her Broadway cast recording of Jule Styne's and Bob Merrill's *Funny Girl* was released the following year, going gold and peaking at Number Two. It is a gorgeous album of show tunes, among its highlights being 'People', 'If A Girl Isn't Pretty Like Miss Atlantic City', 'Don't Rain On My Parade', 'I'm The Greatest Star' and 'You Are Woman, I Am Man'. The exciting songs offered Barbra the opportunity to run through the whole gamut of her range, from funny to yearning to celebratory.

Barbra's fourth solo album, *People*, released in 1964, proved her best yet. She was on form in a fine collection of songs whose highlights include 'People' (reprised from *Funny Girl*), 'Absent Minded Me', 'When In Rome', 'How Does The Wine Taste?', 'Don't Like Goodbyes' and 'Supper Time'. Again, *People* became a gold album, reaching Number One in the US Top 200, and it won Grammy Awards for Best Female Vocals and Best Album Cover.

My Name Is Barbra, released in 1965, picturing Barbra as a child on one cover of the sleeve and as a sophisticated adult on the other, was the recording of the television show. The childhood songs on the first side are very much a matter of taste, and don't bear repeated playing, but the second side is spectacular, with 'Someone To Watch Over Me', 'I've Got No Strings' (from *Pinocchio*) and 'Why Did I Choose You?' The album climaxes with its best track, Barbra's belting rendition of the classic torch song 'My Man'. This gold album reached Number Two in the US Top 200 and won Barbra another Grammy Award for Best Female Vocals. It was followed in the same year by a hasty sequel, *My Name Is Barbra, Two,* highlighted by 'He Touched Me', 'The Shadow Of Your Smile', 'Second Hand Rose' and the climactic medley of seven songs from the *My Name Is Barbra* television show. It went platinum and reached Number Two. Another album of a television show, *Color Me Barbra,* was released in 1966: it went gold and reached Number Three but, with its medley of songs largely (and tenuously) linked by the word 'face',

it seems more a souvenir of the show than an album that can stand on its own.

Je M'Appelle Barbra, in 1966, found the star singing French ballads, with 'What Now My Love?', 'Autumn Leaves' and 'I Wish You Love' as highlights. It reached Number Five in *Billboard*'s charts.

ABOVE: Sophisticated Streisand: Barbra wins a Grammy award.

Simply Streisand, Barbra's 1967 LP of standards – including 'More Than You Know', 'The Boy Next Door', 'Lover Man' and 'My Funny Valentine' – reached Number 12. She then reunited with Jack Gold, co-producer of *Simply Streisand*, to make *A Christmas Album*, which became a massive Yuletide bestseller in 1967. Audiences found

---

'She sings with her customary brilliance on songs like 'Second Hand Rose', 'Cry Me A River', 'Silent Night' and 'People.'
VARIETY ON A HAPPENING IN CENTRAL PARK

---

it hard to resist Barbra's renditions of 'Have Yourself A Merry Little Christmas', 'White Christmas' and 'My Favorite Things', despite their heavy associations with other singers, and the money-spinning album reached Number One and went triple-platinum.

A Happening in Central Park, another television souvenir, although overloaded with too-familiar pieces recorded elsewhere in better studio-produced

versions, went gold and reached Number 30 in 1968. The same year saw Streisand releasing the original soundtrack version of *Funny Girl*; this proved to be a terrific album and, unlike most of its kind, stands up on its own. Jule Styne had penned a couple of new songs for the film, and all the best tunes of the original show are there. Many of the reviewers proclaimed that this album, which went platinum and reached Number 12, was superior to the Broadway recording.

Eager though they were for fresh material, many fans were disappointed with 1969's *What About Today?*, judging it a mediocre studio-produced hotch-potch of contemporary songs like 'Alfie' and 'With A Little Help From My Friends'. It disappointed in the charts too, reaching only Number 31. Back with soundtrack recordings, 1969's *Hello, Dolly!* proved another souvenir album that could more than stand on its own, rewarding constant replaying. Although one of Barbara's finest hours on disc, it reached only Number 49. Vocally she does what she didn't do on film – make the role her own. 'Just Leave Everything To Me', 'So Long Dearie' and 'Before The Parade Goes By' are the main highlights of her zesty work on the Jerry Herman score.

Barbra Streisand's Greatest Hits (1970), her first reprise album, saw critics beginning to wonder just how many repackagings there would be of 'People', 'Don't Rain On My Parade' and 'My Man'. Nonetheless, the album went double-platinum and reached Number 32 in the US charts. Another film soundtrack recording that appeared in the same year, *On a Clear Day You Can See Forever*, failed to make the top 100. As with the movie, this is scarcely an album to relish, despite Barbra's fine renditions of the show's one top song, the title track, and 'Love With All The Trimmings' and 'What Did I Have That I Don't Have?' Yves Montand's singing is hardly bearable.

A further Streisand soundtrack recording, *The Owl and the Pussycat*, appeared in 1971. Consisting merely of dialogue and score – performed by Blood, Sweat and Tears – this just squeezed into the top 200.

By contrast, a new pop-oriented album, *Stoney End*, named after Streisand's Laura Nyro song hit, appeared in 1971 to general acclaim and great popularity, becoming a platinum album and reaching Number Ten. Barbra is outstanding in several fine numbers,

including Joni Mitchell's 'I Don't Know Where I Stand', Randy Newman's 'I'll Be Home' and Harry Nilsson's 'Maybe'. The album was produced by Richard Perry, and he produced also her next, *Barbra Joan Streisand*, again released in 1971. It turned out to be much less thrilling, though among its highlights is an exciting rendition of 'A House Is Not A Home'. This gold album reached Number 11 in the US Top 200.

Another concert souvenir album, *Live Concert at the Forum*, appeared in 1972; naturally Barbra was still belting out

'Don't Rain On My Parade', 'My Man' and 'People'. This platinum album, which hit the Top 20, was followed by yet another television souvenir album, *Barbra Streisand . . . and Other Musical Instruments,* in 1973, which, though ephemeral and dismissed by the critics, is a handy record of the programme.

On the other hand, like *Funny Girl* and *Hello, Dolly*!, the movie-soundtrack recording of *The Way We Were,* released in January 1974, proved one of Barbra's most satisfying experiences on album, and is playable over and over again. The lovely songs by Alan Bergman and Marilyn Bergman include 'The Way We Were', 'Being At War With Each Other', 'The Best Thing You've Ever Done', 'All In Love Is Fair', 'What Are You Doing The Rest Of My Life?', 'Summer Me, Winter Me' and 'How About Me?' The album went gold and reached the US Top 20, winning Grammy Awards for Song of the Year ('The Way We Were') and Best Original Film Score. Released virtually simultaneously was Barbra's solo album *Barbra Streisand: The Way We Were,* containing some new material, which soared to Number One for three weeks in March. The film company Rastar sued Columbia Records for unfair trading, a suit that was settled out of court: the solo album was retitled *Barbra Streisand Featuring The Way We Were and All In Love Is Fair* so that fans wouldn't be confused into thinking it was the soundtrack. 'The Way We Were', released in November 1973, became Barbra's first Number One single.

Butterfly, produced by Jon Peters, was released in 1974 to reasonable reviews and sales, but was a comedown after the heights of *The Way We Were*. It went gold nevertheless, reaching Number 13. Barbra as usual seems often uncomfortable on a pop album, but her misbegotten version of David Bowie's 'Life On Mars', which he is reported to have called 'bloody awful', is balanced by the success of 'Guava Jelly', 'Let The Good Times Roll', 'Love In The Afternoon' and 'Jubilation'.

Repeating another familiar pattern, the 1975 soundtrack album of *Funny Lady* was a tremendous success, with gutsy renditions of a clutch of top Fred Ebb and John Kander show tunes, including 'Let's Hear It for Me' and 'Just How Lucky Can You Get'. The album was her 17th gold disc, and reached *Billboard*'s Number Six slot.

Back in the pop vein, 1975's *Lazy Afternoon* proved popular all round, with

'Shake Me, Wake Me' and 'By the Way' outstanding. Her 18th gold album, it went to Number 12. Then came something completely different: an admirer of and constant listener to classical music, Barbra turned in a new direction with *Classic Barbra*, released in February 1976. This bold album did well enough to reach Number 46 in the pop charts and stayed in the Top Ten in the classical charts for four months. Barbra sings in Italian, German and French and must have been gratified to be rewarded with a Grammy nomination for Best Classical Vocal Solo Performance. 'It doesn't matter what people think of it, what matters is the work itself,' she said.

Returning to familiar territory, the 1976 soundtrack album of *A Star is Born* proved a highlight of her recording career. Both sales and plaudits piled high, and this became a quadruple-platinum album, taking the Number One slot in the United States. Her own hit song, 'Evergreen', was handed a Grammy Award for Song of the Year, and she was honoured as well for Best Female Pop Vocal. Other highlights are 'Watch Closely Now', 'Everything' and 'Lost Inside Of You'.

A Star Is Born won Barbra many new young fans, and she decided to appeal further to them with another pop album, *Streisand Superman*, released in June 1977. The best tracks here proved to be Billy Joel's 'New York State Of Mind', 'Answer Me', 'Love Comes From

ABOVE: *'It doesn't matter what people think of it. What matters is the work itself.'*

Unexpected Places', 'Lullaby For Myself' and the chart single hit 'My Heart Belongs To Me'. Produced by Gary Klein, *Streisand Superman* was a big success: Barbra's second platinum album, it attained Number Three. Klein and Streisand followed up with *Songbird* (1978), which also went platinum,

RIGHT: After the triumph of The Way We Were *the* Los Angeles Times *was disappointed with Streisand's next effort, 'Songbird' is Streisand safely negotiating the lanes to the right of the middle of the road.'*

reaching Number 12. Highlights are the title track and the Grammy-nominated 'You Don't Bring Me Flowers'.

Barbra sang one number, 'Prisoner', on the soundtrack recording of the Jon Peters-produced thriller *Eyes of Laura Mars* in 1978. She apparently refused to take on the star role eventually played by Faye Dunaway because she found the material too violent.

A second ramble down memory lane, *Barbra Streisand's Greatest Hits Volume 2*, released in 1978, hit paydirt in terms of quadruple-platinum sales and the Number One slot. Barbra then released the soundtrack recording of her film *The Main Event* in June 1979. She sang the title number on the LP, which went gold and reached Number 20.

Wet, a third pop album produced by Gary Klein, was released in October 1979. It contains songs of the soggy kind. But Barbra's duet with disco diva Donna Summer, 'No More Tears/Enough Is Enough', proved a showstopper, and yet another Streisand album went platinum, reaching the Top Ten. But the success of this album was easily topped by *Guilty* in 1980. Co-produced by Barry Gibb, who also sang the hit title track and 'What Kind Of Fool' with Barbra, it put her at the pinnacle of pop popularity, going to Number One and achieving quintuple-platinum status. The icing on the cake of the spectacular sales came when Streisand and Gibb won a Grammy for Best Pop Vocal by Duo or Group (for 'Guilty').

Memories, released in 1981, is an uncomfortable mixture of greatest hits and new songs like 'Memory' and 'Coming Out Of Your Life', produced and arranged by Andrew Lloyd Webber. Streisand's beautiful rendition of 'Memory' didn't become a US hit, although Elaine Paige's cover version reached the Top Ten in the UK. Nevertheless, *Memories* remained for two years in the US charts, peaking at Number Six, and became a quadruple-platinum album, while in the UK it reached Number One under the title *Love Songs.*

The lovely Alan Bergman and Marilyn Bergman songs for *Yentl's* soundtrack, released in 1983, scored another Top Ten platinum album for Barbra. The following year's pop album *Emotion* likewise went platinum, but stalled at only Number 19 in the US charts. The latter album includes 'Left In The Dark', Streisand's own 'Here We Are At Last' and a duet with Kim Carnes, 'Make No Mistake He's Mine'.

Disappointed by *Emotion,* Barbra decided to try another change of direction, going back to her show-tune roots to record a series of classic songs, with several by current Broadway maestro Stephen Sondheim. Columbia Records, seeing her as a pop star, advised her against the project, but it was released as *The Broadway Album* in November 1985 (as a single disc, although Barbra had wanted to make a double album). The result, her most successful solo album, went to Number One (her sixth chart topper) and achieved triple-platinum status, taking Grammy Awards for Best Female Pop Vocal and Best Arrangement. The Sondheim numbers, plus Rodgers and Hammerstein's 'If I Loved You' (from *Carousel*), are standouts.

Richard Baskin produced *One Voice,* which contained a clutch of old material and was released in April 1987; it went platinum and reached Number Nine. Next came the pop-oriented *Till I Loved You* (featuring the title duet with Don Johnson) in November 1988; it too went platinum and attained the Top Ten.

A third compilation album, *A Collection: Greatest Hits and More,* appeared in 1989 and enjoyed platinum sales. And there was still more nostalgia when in September 1991 Barbra released *Just for the Record,* a mammoth four-album boxed set containing 95 tracks, 65 of them never before released, including her very first recording, 'You'll Never Know', made at the age of 13. This glorious treat for the fans, though inevitably costly, easily sold a million in the United States and reached Number 38 in the charts.

Barbra sang four numbers for the soundtrack of *The Prince of Tides* in 1991; the album was released to quiet sales, reaching only Number 84. The long-awaited sequel to 1985's *The Broadway Album,* called *Back to Broadway*, appeared in July 1993. This album, her first to go straight to the top slot, includes duets with her one-time *Hello, Dolly!* co-star Michael Crawford ('Music Of The Night') and Johnny Matthis ('One Hand, One Heart'). It is not quite as exciting as the first Broadway album, and it sold fewer, though still going double-platinum.

Streisand's most recent offering is the double-album souvenir of her concert tour, *Barbra: The Concert*, released in September 1994 – another platinum album. Her outstanding vocal performance on 'Ordinary Miracles' earned her one of a brace of Grammy nominations for this album, but this time there were no wins, though she received ample compensation in the shape of that Special Lifetime Achievement Award.